1920—1929

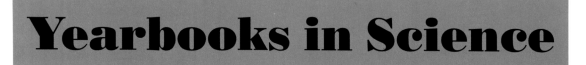

Yearbooks in Science

1920–1929

David E. Newton

Twenty-First Century Books
A Division of Henry Holt and Company
New York

Twenty-First Century Books
A Division of Henry Holt and Company, Inc.
115 West 18th Street
New York, NY 10011

Henry Holt® and colophon are trademarks of
Henry Holt and Company, Inc.
Publishers since 1866

Published in Canada by Fitzhenry & Whiteside Ltd.
195 Allstate Parkway, Markham, Ontario L3R 4T8

Library of Congress Cataloging-in-Publication Data
Yearbooks in science.
p. cm.
Includes indexes.
Contents: 1900–1919 / Tom McGowen — 1920–1929 / David E. Newton — 1930–1939 / Nathan Aaseng — 1940–1949 / Nathan Aaseng — 1950–1959 / Mona Kerby — 1960–1969 / Tom McGowen — 1970–1979 / Geraldine Marshall Gutfreund — 1980–1989 / Robert E. Dunbar — 1990 and beyond / Herma Silverstein.
ISBN 0–8050–3431–5 (v. 1)
1. Science—History—20th century—Juvenile literature. 2. Technology—History—20th century—Juvenile literature. 3. Inventions—History—20th century—Juvenile literature. 4. Scientists—20th century—Juvenile literature. 5. Engineers—20th century—Juvenile literature. [1. Science—History—20th century. 2. Technology—History—20th century.]
Q126.4.Y43 1995
609'.04—dc20   95–17485
                                                          CIP
                                                          AC

ISBN 0–8050–3432–3
First Edition 1995
Printed in Mexico
All first editions are printed on acid-free paper ∞.
10 9 8 7 6 5 4 3 2 1

Cover design by James Sinclair
Interior design by Kelly Soong

Cover photo credits
Background: funeral mask of Tutankhamen, The Bettmann Archive. **Inset images** (clockwise from top right): symbol for the element hafnium; EEG, Photo Researchers, Inc.; Fruit Fly, Comstock; Rorschach inkblot, Custom Medical Stock Photo, Inc.; Peking Man, Tom McHugh/Field Museum, Chicago/Photo Researchers, Inc.

Photo credits
p. 10, 12, 35, 56, 63: UPI/Bettmann; p. 14, 41, 44, 48, 53, 55: The Bettmann Archive; p. 15, 30, 57: Science Photo Library/Photo Researchers, Inc.; p. 17: North Wind Picture Archives; p. 19: Michael Freeman/Phototake, NYC; p. 20: AIP/Emilio Segre Visual Archives/Francis Simon Collection; p. 22: AIP/Emilio Segre Visual Archives/Goudsmit Collection; p. 23: AIP/Emilio Segre Visual Archives; p. 28: Novosti/SPL/Photo Researchers, Inc.; p. 31: Dr. Dennis Kunkel/Phototake, NYC; p. 37: A. B. Dowsett/SPL/Photo Researchers, Inc.; p. 40: Erich Schrempp/Photo Researchers, Inc.; p. 42: Marvy!/The Stock Market; p. 46: Monkmeyer/Forsyth; p. 47: Comstock; p. 50: John Reader/SPL/Photo Researchers, Inc.; p. 51: Tom McHugh/Field Museum, Chicago/Photo Researchers, Inc.; p. 60: John Sanford/SPL/Photo Researchers, Inc.; p. 61: Science Source/Photo Researchers, Inc.; p. 68: C. Powell, P. Fowler & D. Perkins/SPL/Photo Researchers, Inc.

To Ann Crispin Hedberg, for her many contributions to the field and, more important, for being such a dependable friend!

Contents

1

PHYSICS

The 1920s was a decade of dramatic upheaval in physics. Fundamental concepts that had seemed indisputable for more than 400 years had begun to crumble in the first two decades of the twentieth century. By the end of the 1920s, physicists had created new and strikingly different ways of looking at the nature of matter and energy.

WAVE-PARTICLE DUALITY

Among the most basic of these changes was the disappearance of the distinction between matter and energy. At the end of the nineteenth century, any physicist could confidently have defined matter as the "stuff" of which the universe is made and energy as the "drive" that brings about changes in matter. No one would have confused one of these concepts with the other.

Max Planck's discovery of the quantum of energy in 1900 was the first crack in this traditional separation of matter and energy. The term *quantum* refers to a particlelike "package" of energy. Before 1900, scientists believed that energy could be described as a wavelike motion, somewhat similar to water waves, and matter could be described as a collection of tiny particles known as atoms and molecules. Planck developed a mathematical theory in which energy could be viewed in a new way, as a stream of tiny, atomlike particles that he called quanta.

The quantum theory was greatly strengthened in 1905 when Albert Einstein used Planck's ideas to explain the photoelectric effect. Then, in 1923, the first concrete evidence for the existence of the quantum was reported.

Working at the University of Chicago, the American physicist Arthur Holly Compton bombarded crystals with X rays. He found that the wave-

Arthur Holly Compton's work convinced other scientists that X rays have both a wavelike and a particlelike nature.

length of X rays increased when they were reflected off crystals. What did this discovery mean? Compton knew that the energy of an X ray depends on its wavelength: the longer the wavelength, the less energy the X ray has. His experiment had shown, therefore, that an X ray loses energy when it reflects off a crystal.

Compton suggested that this phenomenon, now called the Compton effect, could be explained by assuming that X rays consist of tiny quanta of energy, like those described by Planck and Einstein. Compton proposed the name *photon* for this quantum of energy, a name that was later adopted and is still used today. When an X-ray photon strikes a crystal, Compton said, it loses energy and rebounds as a photon of lesser energy—a photon of longer wavelength.

Compton's success in writing precise equations to describe this event convinced scientists that electromagnetic radiation like X rays has both a wavelike and particlelike nature. For this discovery of wave-particle duality, Compton was awarded a share of the 1927 Nobel Prize in physics.

The Planck-Einstein-Compton concept of energy quanta was not an entirely new idea. As early as the 1670s, Sir Isaac Newton had suggested that light may consist of particles. But the opposite possibility—that matter might have energylike properties—was an entirely new concept when it was first suggested by French physicist Prince Louis de Broglie in 1924.

De Broglie was convinced that if energy could sometimes behave like matter, then matter must also sometimes have the properties of energy. He used theoretical principles developed by Planck and Einstein to write a mathematical equation showing that a moving particle travels in a wavelike pattern.

The de Broglie equation shows that large particles moving at a relatively slow velocity (like a batted baseball) have a wavelength so small that it could probably never be measured. But very small particles traveling at very high velocities—like an electron in an atom—have wavelengths in the electromagnetic region that can rather easily be measured. In fact, only three years after de Broglie announced his theory, it was confirmed experimentally by the American physicists Clinton Joseph Davisson and Lester Halbert Germer.

Davisson and Germer made their discovery while bombarding a piece of nickel metal with a beam of electrons. They found that electrons reflected off the metal formed a diffraction pattern. A diffraction pattern is a design formed when waves are bent by some object placed in their path. Water flowing around a rock in the middle of a stream often produces a rippling effect that is a diffraction pattern.

But diffraction is a property of waves, not particles. It must be, Davisson and Germer concluded, that their beam of electrons was traveling as a wave, just as de Broglie had predicted. Only a few months later, the English physicist George Paget Thomson observed the same diffraction of electrons as they passed through gold foil.

These results raised difficult new questions for physicists. How can we know when something is a particle (matter) or a wave (energy)? In using a

Dr. Clinton J. Davisson, shown here, shared the 1937 Nobel Prize in physics with George P. Thomson of London.

beam of X rays, for example, should we think of the X rays as a wave of energy or as quanta? The answer physicists have developed is: you decide! A researcher chooses the model—wave or particle—that works best for the setting in which she or he is working. Most phenomena in the natural world apparently have a two-sided character (duality), and a scientist can choose which side he or she wants to consider in his or her own work. The discoveries of de Broglie, Davisson, Thomson, and their colleagues on the duality of matter and energy thus provided scientists with a new and fascinating way of viewing the natural world.

QUANTUM MECHANICS

Perhaps the most difficult challenge faced by physicists in the mid-1920s was to find new methods for dealing with new physical concepts such as the quantum of energy and particle waves. Familiar mathematical systems such as algebra, geometry, and calculus were simply inadequate for analyzing these revolutionary new ideas.

One new approach was suggested by the German physicist Werner Heisenberg. Heisenberg argued that physicists should give up trying to imagine what a quantum of energy or an electron wave looks like. It was no longer possible, he said, to develop theories based on *physical* models. Instead, he suggested that physicists rely entirely on *mathematical* data—boiling points, freezing points, densities, indexes of refraction, and the like—in building their theories. The task, he said, was to discover what new information could be discovered working only with these quantitative data.

In 1925, Heisenberg worked out a new (he thought) form of mathematics by which this kind of analysis could be done. Data were arranged in a matrix consisting of rows and columns like a teacher's grade book. Heisenberg then developed a set of rules by which these numbers could be manipulated to give answers to equations. He called the system matrix mechanics.

Werner Heisenberg was awarded the Nobel Prize in Physics in 1932 for his application of matrix mechanics to physical phenomena.

When Heisenberg showed his ideas to his colleague at the University of Göttingen, Max Born, Born pointed out that Heisenberg's "new" idea was actually a technique well known to mathematicians, called matrix mathematics. The rules Heisenberg had developed were all part of a well-developed system familiar to all mathematicians and many physicists.

Nonetheless, Heisenberg's application of matrix mathematics to physical phenomena was a startling breakthrough. It provided interesting predictions about the nature of matter based on new physical principles such as wave-particle duality. In November 1925, Heisenberg, Born, and another colleague, Pascual Jordan, published a detailed description of the use of matrix mechanics to solve physical problems. At last, physicists had one of the new tools they had been looking for.

At about the same time, the Austrian physicist Erwin Schrödinger was working on another method for solving problems involving energy quanta and particle waves. Having just read about de Broglie's concept of particle waves, Schrödinger asked himself why he couldn't write a mathematical equation that would describe the wave motion of an electron. Physicists had been writing equations for sound waves, light waves, and other kinds of waves for hundreds of years. But writing an equation for an electron traveling as a wave was a new and challenging task.

By January of 1926, however, Schrödinger announced that he had achieved success. He had found a set of complicated equations that accurately described the motion of an electron as it travels around the nucleus of an atom. Remarkably, the predictions made by Schrödinger's wave equation were almost exactly the same as those hypothesized by Niels Bohr thirteen years earli-

Erwin Schrödinger's wave equation gave a mathematical picture of the arrangement of electrons in an atom.

er. But Bohr had come up with his theory by studying the results of experiments, while Schrödinger had developed his ideas purely by the use of mathematics. Experiment and theory had come together with an identical picture of the arrangement of electrons in an atom!

For a period of time, physicists were confused as to which method—Heisenberg's matrix mechanics or Schrödinger's wave mechanics—they should use to solve problems. Most preferred Schrödinger's technique since it was based on a concrete physical model that they could understand. They were less comfortable with the abstract mathematics of matrix mechanics.

As it turned out, the choice between matrix and wave mechanics eventually became a nonproblem. In 1944, the Hungarian-American mathematician John von Neumann showed that the two methods are mathematically equivalent to each other. Use of either one will result in a correct analysis of any given problem.

From the late 1920s to the present day, then, physical problems at the atomic level have been studied by a new form of mathematics generally known as quantum mechanics.

THE UNCERTAINTY PRINCIPLE

In spite of his important work on matrix mechanics, Heisenberg is far better known in connection with a second discovery he made in the 1920s, the uncertainty principle. Most people probably think of scientific knowledge in terms of *certainty*. Scientists, the general public tends to believe, deal with cold, hard, definite facts. And, until the 1920s, scientists themselves essentially agreed with that viewpoint. They were confident that they could accurately and precisely discover the melting point of a metal, the velocity of a falling object, the position of an electron in an atom, and any other physical phenomenon.

In 1927, Heisenberg showed that this view of nature and science could no longer be defended. Imagine, he said, that a scientist wants to find the location of an electron in an atom. One way to do that might be to shine light on the electron in order to "see" where it is (with a very high-powered microscope). But an electron is so small and light that its position would be disturbed by the force of the light wave striking it. What the scientist would actually "see" would be not the electron's *actual* position in the atom, but its position after having been struck by the light wave.

In general, Heisenberg said, the very act of measuring an object or event disturbs that object or event, preventing an absolutely unhindered determination of its properties.

The Heisenberg uncertainty effect is very small for phenomena in our everyday lives. The "disturbing" effect of measuring the length of a board is so small compared to the size of the board that it is insignificant. The effect of such a measurement on the atomic scale, however, is significant. In fact, it must always be taken into consideration when thinking about electrons, atoms, and other very small particles.

The effect of Heisenberg's discovery of the uncertainty principle has been profound. Scientists have had to develop a whole new language in talking about physical phenomena. They can no longer say that they "know" some things for sure. Instead, they must express a degree of confidence that some measurement may or may not be correct.

Heisenberg's discovery has had important implications far beyond the field of science. One of early modern science's major contributions to human thought was the concept of cause and effect: we can discover, scientists taught us, that B happens because A caused it to happen. For example, we know that light and water cause plants to grow.

The uncertainty principle means that humans have to think about events—and not just those in the scientific world—in terms of *probability* rather than certainty. Instead of stating absolute truths in terms of assurance, it may be necessary at times to think about the *likelihood* (high or low) that some concept may actually be true.

ATOMIC THEORY

The focus of nearly every major development in physics in the 1920s was atomic theory. Quantum mechanics, wave-particle duality, the uncertainty principle, and other new concepts were all employed to create a striking new view of the atom's structure.

The pace of change in atomic theory was remarkable. In 1895, scientists still tended to think of the atom in terms first suggested by the English scientist John Dalton nearly a century before, in 1803, as a tiny, solid, indivisible

John Dalton, often called the father of modern atomic theory

particle. Three decades later, they were just beginning to recognize that the best way to visualize the atom was probably not in physical terms at all, but as a set of mathematical equations that described the characteristics of the electrons in an atom and their interaction with the atomic nucleus.

Niels Bohr had provided the great breakthrough in atomic theory in 1913. He had suggested that the atom could be thought of as a tiny system something like our solar system. The nucleus of the atom was at the center of that system, and the atom's electrons orbited around the nucleus, just as the planets orbit around the sun.

The mathematical theory that Bohr developed to describe this solar systemlike atom required the use of a new concept, a quantum number, which told where the electrons were in an atom. Electrons in the first orbit around the atom's nucleus were assigned a quantum number of 1, those in the second orbit around the nucleus had a quantum number of 2, those in the third orbit, a quantum number of 3, and so on.

The Bohr model was a remarkable success in explaining many of the most obvious features of the structure of matter. Scientists were delighted in having been given the best description of atoms in history. Still, they knew almost immediately that the Bohr theory was not perfect. The solar system atom was not successful in explaining every precise detail that was known about matter. The search for an even more refined picture of the atom continued.

The next breakthrough came in 1916 when the Austrian physicist Arnold Sommerfeld suggested a modification of the Bohr model. Suppose, he said, that electrons travel around the nucleus not in circles, as Bohr had said, but in ellipses. An ellipse is a flattened circle that looks something like the outer shell of an egg. Sommerfeld introduced a second quantum number, known as the secondary or azimuthal quantum number (l) to describe the flatness of an electron's orbit. Shortly thereafter, scientists found that yet a third quantum number, describing the way the magnetic field of an electron interacts with the magnetic field of the nucleus, was also necessary to complete the description of the atom. This quantum number was called the magnetic quantum number, or m_l.

In 1920, therefore, scientists had a more complete understanding of the atom than was the case only seven years earlier. But, as they soon discovered, the picture was not yet complete. The final piece of the quantum number puzzle was provided by the Austrian-American physicist Wolfgang Pauli in 1925.

Pauli was working on a puzzle that dated back to 1896. In that year, the Dutch physicist Pieter Zeeman had conducted experiments on the production of spectra in the presence of magnetic fields. The word *spectrum* (plural: *spectra*) refers to the rainbow of colors produced when light passes through a glass prism. When an element such as carbon or iron is heated until it glows, the light produced forms not a continuous, rainbowlike spectrum, but one that consists of very narrow lines, a line spectrum.

In Zeeman's experiments, elements were heated to glowing in a strong magnetic field. Under these conditions, Zeeman found that each of the lines in a line spectrum broke into two parts, called doublets. Pauli eventually found that this effect could be explained if an electron had some fourth fundamental property that could be specified by a fourth quantum number. Pauli

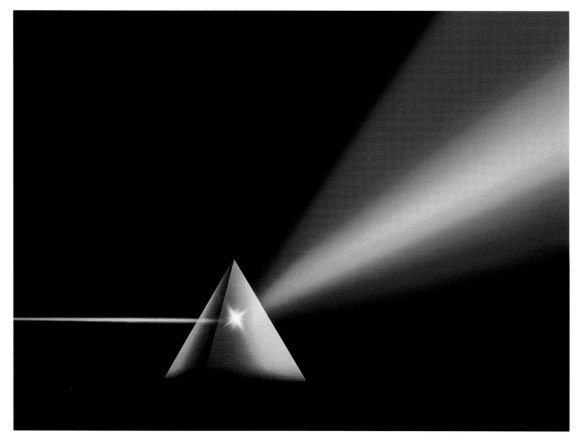

Light passing through a prism creates a spectrum of color.

had no idea what that fourth property was, but he did know that, mathematically, it could have only two possible values, $+\frac{1}{2}$ or $-\frac{1}{2}$.

With a full set of quantum numbers now, Pauli made a remarkable discovery. Suppose, he said, that one calculates the sets of quantum numbers allowed by the Schrödinger wave equation and other formulas that apply to the electrons in an atom. According to these equations, as an example, if $n = 2$ (that is, if we are talking about electrons in the second orbital), then *mathematically* it follows that l can have values of 1 and 0 only and m_l can be only $+1$, -1, or 0. With two possible values for the fourth quantum number ($+\frac{1}{2}$ or $-\frac{1}{2}$), one can then write eight sets of quantum numbers:

2, 1, $+1$, $+\frac{1}{2}$; 2, 1, $+1$, $-\frac{1}{2}$; 2, 1, -1, $+\frac{1}{2}$ and so on.

Now, Pauli said, suppose that no two electrons in an atom can have exactly the same set of quantum numbers. That is, only one electron can have the set 2, 1, $+1$, $+\frac{1}{2}$; only one can have the set 2, 1, $+1$, $-\frac{1}{2}$; and so on.

Wolfgang Pauli's work with electrons provided the final piece of the quantum number puzzle.

Then, for the second orbital in an atom ($n = 2$), there can be only eight electrons. Those eight electrons would have the following quantum numbers:

2, 1, +1, +½; 2, 1, +1, -½; 2, 1, 0, +½; 2, 1, 0, -½; 2, 1, -1, +½; 2, 1, -1, -½; 2, 0, 0, +½; 2, 0, 0, -½.

Pauli went on to calculate the number of electrons that could exist in other orbitals, using this exclusion principle. He found that his results exactly matched those hypothesized by Niels Bohr in 1913 based on experimental evidence, but with no theoretical basis. For example, in the third orbital ($n = 3$), Pauli found the same 18 electrons Bohr had predicted. These 18 electrons had quantum numbers such as:

3, 2, +1, +½; 3, 2, +1, -½; 3, 2, 0, +½; 3, 2, 0, -½; 3, 2, -1, +½; 3, 2, -1, -½;

and so on through all 18 possible sets of quantum numbers with $n = 3$.

Pauli had finally established a sound theoretical explanation for the atomic model that physicists had been developing for over a decade.

The happy conclusion to Pauli's work came in 1928. In that year, two Dutch graduate students, Samuel Goudsmit and George Uhlenbeck, discovered that an electron spins on its own axis. The two possible directions of spin—clockwise and counterclockwise—explain the two possible values of Pauli's fourth quantum number, +½ and -½.

As the 1920s drew to a close, one nagging question about atomic theory continued to trouble physicists. Existing models did not take into consideration the effects of relativity. In 1905, Einstein had introduced his special theory of relativity, showing that the measurements made on a particle were influenced by the speed with which that particle was moving. Physicists understood that a complete and accurate theory of the atom had to take into account relativistic effects caused by the motion of electrons around the atomic nucleus. But the mathematics of dealing with such effects were very difficult. As a result, most physicists used nonrelativistic mathematics in their atomic models, and then simply acknowledged that defect in their work.

In 1928, however, the brilliant English physicist Paul A. M. Dirac remedied this problem. He revised existing equations for the atom to include the effects of relativity. In the process, he made a remarkable discovery. His cal-

Samuel Goudsmit (right) and George Uhlenbeck (left) discovered electron spin, thus explaining the two possible values of the fourth quantum number.

culations showed that electrons could have either a positive or negative energy. But how could an electron—or anything else—have less-than-zero (negative) energy?

Dirac's solution to this puzzle was to hypothesize the existence of an antielectron, a particle identical in every respect to an ordinary electron except for its having a positive charge rather than a negative charge. That prediction was a bold one indeed and one that many physicists regarded as

Paul A. M. Dirac predicted the existence of an antielectron, a prediction that was proven to be true fours years later.

an absurdity. Yet only four years after Dirac announced his hypothesis of the antielectron, that particle was discovered by the American physicist Carl David Anderson, who named the particle the positron.

ARTIFICIAL TRANSMUTATION OF THE ELEMENTS

Most of the advances described thus far were in the area of theoretical physics. But important changes were also under way in the field of experimental physics. Among the most significant of these were successes in converting one element into another by means of nuclear reactions.

During the Middle Ages, a number of scholars had looked for ways to change lead into gold. These scholars were called alchemists. They were not really scientists, but they helped set the stage for the science that we know today as chemistry. The alchemists believed that lead was an "immature" kind of metal and gold a "mature" kind of metal. If they could find a way to make lead "grow up" very quickly, the alchemists thought, they could become very rich.

By the twentieth century, scientists no longer believed that lead could be changed into gold. In the 1920s, however, the idea of converting one element into another began to reemerge as a real possibility. That possibility came about as the result of pioneering work by Ernest Rutherford and James Chadwick at Cambridge University's Cavendish Laboratory in England.

Rutherford's first success in this line of research—changing one substance into another—had been achieved in 1919 when he used alpha particles (helium atoms that have lost their electrons) from naturally radioactive materials to bombard a sample of nitrogen gas in a glass tube. He found that protons were ejected in the process, leaving behind oxygen gas in the tube. Over the next five years, Rutherford and Chadwick repeated this experiment with fifteen more elements, obtaining a transmutation (change) in each case.

Further research on the conversion of one element to another awaited development in technology, however. Machinery had to be developed that would accelerate alpha particles—and other elementary particles such as protons and electrons—to high velocities. With such velocities, the particle could collide with atomic nuclei and bring about many new types of nuclear reactions. In 1929, the first experimental machine of this type was put into operation by John Cockroft and Ernest Walton at Cambridge. The discoveries to be made with this and similar machines would further shake the foundations of physics in the 1930s.

2

CHEMISTRY

One body of chemical research during the 1920s was aimed along traditional lines, attempting to discover any remaining new elements, finding out more about the nature of isotopes (different forms of a single element), and working out a better understanding of solutions, such as seawater and sugar water. But revolutionary changes were also beginning to take place. Most important, the historic boundaries between chemistry and physics on the one hand, and chemistry and the life sciences on the other, were beginning to dissolve.

THE SEARCH FOR ELEMENTS

The search for element number 72 has been called "one of chemistry's most controversial episodes." Dmitri Mendeléev's discovery of the periodic law in the late 1860s strongly suggested that only a limited number of chemical elements exist. As a result of his work in the early 1910s, the English physicist Henry Moseley had confirmed Mendeléev's prediction and showed that no more than seven elements remained to be discovered. In 1917, one of those elements, protoactinium, was discovered by the German scientists Lise Meitner and Otto Hahn. Thus, as the 1920s began, only six elements remained to be found.

In 1911, the French chemist Georges Urbain, an authority on the rare-earth elements (a group of elements that occur together in nature and are quite difficult to study), had claimed to have discovered one of these elements, number 72, in a mixture of rare earths. He gave the new element the name *celtium*. Although Urbain later provided additional proof of his discovery, many chemists remained suspicious of his claims. Based on its position

Dmitri Mendeléev proposed a system for classifying the chemical elements that is still in use today — the periodic table.

in the periodic table, element 72 should have chemical properties similar to those of zirconium, located just above it in the table. There seemed to be no reason why number 72 would be associated with the rare-earth elements.

Following up on this line of reasoning, Niels Bohr suggested a new search for element 72 in 1922. He recommended to György Hevesy, a Hungarian chemist, and Dirk Coster, a Dutch physicist, both working with him at the time at the University of Copenhagen, Denmark, that they look for element 72 in zirconium ores (the earthy materials from which zirconium metal is obtained). Within a year, Hevesy and Coster were successful. Using the newly developed technique of X-ray analysis, they were able to detect the suspected element in Norwegian zircon, an ore of zirconium. Hevesy and Coster gave the new element the name *hafnium*, in honor of the Latin name for Copenhagen, Hafnia. They also found that the element is not especially rare, but is difficult to recognize because of its close association with the far more abundant zirconium.

Hevesy and Coster's work showed that Urbain's original claims for element 72 were wrong. Thus, his proposed name for the element, celtium, was rejected.

The second element found during the 1920s was rhenium, discovered in 1925 by the German chemists Ida Eve Tacke, Walter Noddack, and Otto Berg. (Miss Tacke became Mrs. Noddack a year later.) The researchers used X-ray analysis, just as Hevesy and Coster had, to identify the missing element number 75 in a sample of gadolinite, a mineral that contains beryllium, iron, silicon, oxygen, lanthanum, and other elements. They named the element rhenium after the Rhine River.

The Noddacks also claimed to have discovered another of the missing elements, number 43. They named this element masurium after a region in

East Prussia. Efforts by other chemists to validate this claim failed, however. It was not until 1937 that the element was actually found. Then, it was not discovered in nature at all, but it was produced artificially in an experiment carried out in a cyclotron.

As the 1920s drew to a close, therefore, all but four elements had been discovered: 43, 61, 85, and 87. Since no stable form of any one of these elements exists in nature, they were finally discovered in later years only as the result of artificial processes such as the use of a cyclotron or an atomic pile.

IDENTIFICATION OF ISOTOPES

In 1920, the concept of isotopes was still fairly new to chemists and physicists. Although Frederick Soddy had proposed the concept of isotopes—two forms of an element with different atomic weights—as early as 1913, experimental proof for their existence had been provided only in 1919. In that year, the English physicist Francis Aston had invented the mass spectrometer, which showed without doubt that stable as well as radioactive (unstable) isotopes exist.

During the 1920s, Aston continued his search for isotopes among the elements, eventually discovering 212 of the 287 stable isotopes known to exist. In addition, he eventually found that the masses of isotopes are not exact whole numbers. The mass of the nitrogen-14 isotope, for example, is not 14.0000, but 14.0067. The slight variations above and below a whole-number value were later shown to be the result of energy required to hold atomic nuclei together. Two decades later, this information was put to practical use in the development of fission ("atomic") bombs, weapons in which that binding energy is released through the process of nuclear fission.

A second discovery early in the 1920s also proved to be critical in the later development of atomic energy. In 1921, the German chemist Otto Hahn discovered a new isotope of uranium with a mass of 235. He originally called the isotope uranium Z. Uranium-235 makes up only 0.35 percent of natural uranium but is important because of its ability to undergo nuclear fission. The most serious technical problem in producing nuclear weapons in the 1940s was finding a way to separate uranium-235 from its far more abundant but much less valuable cousin, uranium-238.

Otto Hahn is shown here with a colleague, Lise Meitner. The two worked together bombarding uranium with neutrons.

The last year of the decade was marked by another important discovery in the field of isotope research. Working at the University of California at Berkeley, the American chemist William Giauque discovered that at least three isotopes of oxygen, with masses of 16, 17, and 18, exist. This news had at least two major consequences.

In the first place, it raised questions about the system that scientists had been using to specify atomic weights. Until Giauque's discovery, the standard for atomic weights had been to set the atomic weight of oxygen at 16.0000 and then calculate the weights of all other elements based on that standard. But the discovery of oxygen-17 (with an abundance of 0.037 percent) and oxygen-18 (with an abundance of 0.200 percent) meant that the atomic weights of all other elements were slightly incorrect.

One solution suggested for this problem was to set a new standard for atomic weights with oxygen-16 (not normal oxygen) at 16.0000. To do so meant recalculating the atomic weights of all other elements. The solution that was eventually accepted, however, was to set the atomic weight of carbon-12 at 12.0000 as the standard for atomic weights. That system is the one used by chemists and physicists today.

A second consequence of Giauque's discovery was the development of a technique for using the heaviest isotope of oxygen, oxygen-18, as a tracer in scientific studies. A tracer is a substance whose presence in some type of change can be detected and monitored. Since oxygen-18 is 1.125 times as heavy as the far more abundant oxygen-16, it can easily be followed through various biological, chemical, and physical processes. In fact, the use of oxygen-18 as a tracer made possible the discovery in the 1940s of the detailed roles of water and carbon dioxide in the process of photosynthesis.

SOLUTION CHEMISTRY

The behavior of substances in solution had long been an intriguing puzzle to chemists. As an example, a solid crystal of sodium chloride will not conduct an electrical current. But a solution made by dissolving that same

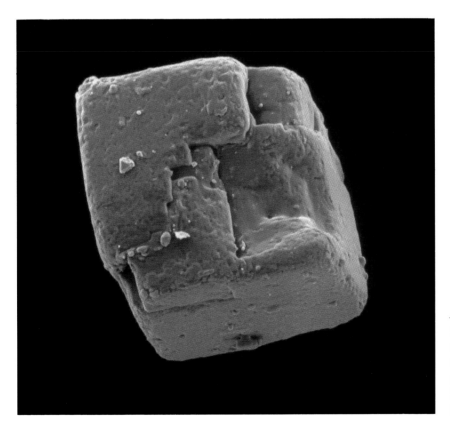

Arrhenius studied crystals, like this crystal of sodium chloride (table salt), in order to develop his theory of ionization.

crystal in water will conduct a current. An apparent explanation for that puzzle was offered in 1884 when the Swedish chemist Svante Arrhenius proposed the theory of ionization. When crystals are dissolved in water, Arrhenius said, they dissociate (break apart) into positive and negative parts (ions) that are then able to carry an electrical current.

Even four decades later, however, Arrhenius's explanation was not entirely satisfactory. Experimental evidence showed clearly that crystals seem not to dissociate completely in solution. The conductivity of such solutions typically ranges from as low as 50 percent to as high as 90 to 100 percent. Yet X-ray analysis shows that the atoms in a crystal are already completely ionized even in the solid state. When placed into water, then, how could they *not* become totally dissociated?

A solution to this puzzle was suggested in 1923 by the Dutch-American physicist Peter Debye. What happens during the dissolving process, he said, is that each positive ion becomes surrounded by a cloud of negative ions, and each negative ion by a cloud of positive ions. Each type of ion is, therefore, somewhat insulated from other ions in the solution, and the degree of dissociation *appears* to be less than 100 percent.

Working with a colleague, Erich A. A. J. Hückel, Debye devised a set of mathematical equations that describe the interaction of positive and negative ions in a solution. These equations are still used to solve many problems involving the properties of solutions.

A specific feature of solution chemistry that had also intrigued chemists for decades was the question of acids and bases. The fundamental theory of acids and bases was also outlined by Arrhenius. He proposed that an acid be defined as any substance that produces hydrogen ions in solution, and a base as any substance that yields hydroxide ions in solution.

As an example, suppose the gas hydrogen chloride is dissolved in water. In water, hydrogen chloride molecules break apart to form hydrogen ions and chloride ions. Since hydrogen ions are formed in this example, hydrogen chloride would be considered (according to Arrhenius) an acid.

For four decades, Arrhenius's definitions worked well enough for chemists. Then, in 1923, the Danish chemist Johannes Nicolaus Brønsted proposed a new way of thinking about acids and bases. Brønsted suggested that acids and bases be defined in terms of the loss and gain of protons. A proton is exactly the same thing as a hydrogen ion. So although Brønsted used a new *term* (proton) in talking about acids and bases, he used the same *concept* as had Arrhenius.

Suppose, Brønsted said, that an acid is defined as any substance that donates (gives away or loses) protons. Then, a Brønsted acid is exactly the same as an Arrhenius acid. In the hydrogen chloride example from above, hydrogen chloride is an acid by either definition because in water it loses (donates) a hydrogen ion (proton) to the water.

But then Brønsted suggested a new definition for a base. Let's define as a base, he said, anything that accepts *protons*. This change was very important since a base was no longer to be thought of in terms of hydroxide ions (as with Arrhenius), but in terms of protons (or hydrogen ions).

The important new feature of the Brønsted theory is that acids and bases always occur together. If one substance (an acid) *donates* a proton, a second substance (the base) must be around to *accept* the proton.

Again, consider the example of hydrogen chloride in water. When gaseous hydrogen chloride is dissolved in water, the hydrogen ions (protons) it loses do not just float around freely in the water. Instead, each proton attaches itself to a water molecule, forming something called a hydronium ion. In this case, hydrogen chloride is the acid because it donates a proton. But water is the base because it accepts that proton. Brønsted referred to an acid-base system such as this one as a conjugate acid-base system.

The Brønsted system became popular among chemists for two reasons. First, it more accurately describes the changes that actually take place within solutions. Second, it expands the meaning of acids and bases. For example, although water would normally not be considered a base by the Arrhenius definition, it could be thought of in that way by the Brønsted system.

CHEMICAL BOND THEORY

During the first two decades of the twentieth century, chemists had struggled with the question of how two atoms combine with each other. In the late 1910s, Gilbert Newton Lewis and Irving Langmuir independently developed theories that showed how the exchange of electrons between two atoms can result in the formation of an ionic or a covalent bond. The 1920s then saw the development of a far more sophisticated analysis of the chemical bond, an analysis based on developments that had taken place in physics.

A handful of chemists began to ask what the consequences of wave-particle duality, relativity, uncertainty, quantum mechanics, and other new concepts were for chemical bond theory. In 1927, two German physicists, Walter Heitler and Fritz London, worked out a mathematical description of the chemical bond between two hydrogen atoms, using quantum mechanics. Their results were a remarkable accomplishment, providing an exact description of all known properties of the hydrogen molecule.

Relatively few chemists, however, were able to fully understand or make use of Heitler and London's work. Their own training seldom included any study of concepts in the "new physics." One exception to this statement was Linus Pauling, a brilliant American chemist who was studying quantum mechanics in Europe at the time of Heitler and London's work. Pauling realized that quantum mechanics was a powerful tool for studying the chemical bond. He made it his professional goal to determine as completely as possible everything that the "new physics" could reveal about the chemical bond. The final result of Pauling's research was his monumental book *The Nature of the Chemical Bond*, published in 1939. The book is widely regarded as one of the greatest texts in the history of chemistry.

The primary consequence of the work done by Heitler, London, and Pauling in the 1920s was to chip away the traditional barriers between physics and chemistry. After this period, no chemist could be considered to be properly trained unless she or he also had at least some grounding in the principles of modern physics.

TETRAETHYL LEAD AS A KNOCK INHIBITOR

The 1920s was a decade of rapid growth in the automotive industry. A chemical discovery that contributed significantly to that growth was tetraethyl lead. Primitive internal combustion engines ran well enough on gasoline obtained directly from the fractional distillation of crude oil ("straight-run" gasoline). But as engines became more sophisticated, they tended to "knock" when operated on straight-run gasoline. This "knocking" resulted in a serious loss of engine efficiency. In 1921, the American chemist Thomas Midgley Jr. found that adding tetraethyl lead to gasoline greatly reduced knocking. Over the next seventy years, the compound became the single most widely used gasoline additive in the world.

Dr. Linus Pauling's contributions to science spanned several decades.

ADVANCES IN THE CHEMISTRY OF LIVING SYSTEMS

The chemical study of compounds found in living organisms was still in its infancy in 1920. Two major reasons accounted for this situation. In the first place, most scientists still regarded life as a special kind of entity with properties that could not be entirely analyzed in the laboratory. One might study one compound or another from a plant or animal, but the whole organism was still regarded as more than a combination of the parts of which it was made. In addition, the compounds found in living organisms are usually far more complex and difficult to analyze than are those found in the nonliving world.

But the 1920s saw a number of breakthroughs in the study of biological chemicals, breakthroughs that were eventually to dissolve the distinction between chemistry and biology. One of those breakthroughs occurred in 1921 with the work on glutathione by the English chemist Sir Frederick Gowland Hopkins. Glutathione is an amino acid, one of the building blocks from which proteins are made. A longtime student of amino acids, Hopkins isolated glutathione from tissue and found that it consists of three amino acids joined to one another. He then went on to show how the gain and loss of hydrogen atoms by glutathione is responsible for chemical changes that take place within cells, changes by which energy is released. This discovery was among the first steps in unraveling the crucial but complex process of cell metabolism. The quest to understand cell metabolism continues to the present day.

The 1920s was also a decade of enormous progress in the study of enzymes. Enzymes are chemicals that occur in living organisms and that make possible most of the chemical reactions on which life depends. For example, when you eat a hamburger, various enzymes in your body break down the bread, meat, lettuce, tomato, and other parts of the hamburger to produce chemicals your body can use.

In the first decades of the twentieth century, scientists had become quite convinced that enzymes are a kind of protein, but they knew little more about them. The first important step forward in the study of enzymes during the 1920s was really a rediscovery. In 1904, the English chemist Arthur Harden had shown that enzymes consist of two parts, both of which are necessary to bring about a chemical change. For two decades, that discovery was largely ignored by most chemists. In 1923, however, the German chemist Hans von Euler-Chelpin picked up on Harden's line of research and discovered the nonprotein part of the enzyme, the co-factor, or co-enzyme. Von Euler-Chelpin was able to determine the molecular weight of the co-enzyme, its chemical structure, and its role in certain cellular reactions. For their study of enzyme structure and function, Harden and von Euler-Chelpin were jointly awarded the 1929 Nobel Prize in chemistry.

A second Nobel Prize in chemistry (given in 1946) was awarded for another line of research on enzymes conducted in the 1920s. That research was carried out by James Sumner, an American chemist. In his experiments, Sumner extracted an enzyme known as urease from a common plant called the jack bean. In the human body, urease breaks down the compound urea, changing it into ammonia and carbon dioxide.

When Sumner made a highly concentrated solution of urease, he observed that tiny crystals began to settle out of the solution. He removed these crystals, redissolved them in water, and then tested their action on urea. He found that the crystals behaved in exactly the same way as did urease itself. From this, he concluded that the tiny crystals were actually crystals of the enzyme itself. Sumner's work provided the first concrete proof that enzymes are clearly identifiable chemical compounds that can be studied in the laboratory like compounds that come from nonliving sources.

In some ways, the most impressive accomplishment in biochemistry during the 1920s was the German chemist Hans Fischer's determination of the chemical structure of heme. At the beginning of his research, in 1921, Fischer had only the most general information about this important substance: its chemical formula, its presence in hemoglobin (the large molecule that makes blood red), and its biological function (the transport of oxygen from the lungs to cells). Over the next decade, he concentrated on finding the one chemical formula among more than a dozen that would fit all the data on heme he could find.

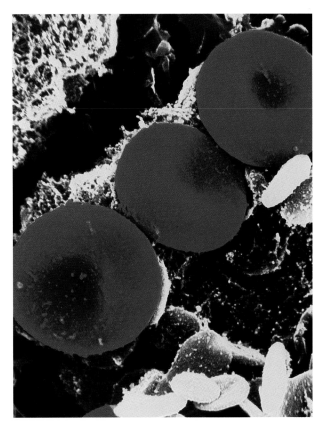

Hans Fischer determined the chemical structure of heme, which is present in red blood cells.

In 1929, Fischer reported the results of that investigation. The seventy-six atoms in heme are arranged, he announced, in one large ring to which four smaller rings are attached. Extending off this central core of rings are eight side chains of three different types. For this long and extremely complex research, Fischer was awarded the 1930 Nobel Prize in chemistry.

Fischer's research marked a further blurring of the lines between biology and chemistry. Scientists were beginning to see that a biological process (the transport of oxygen in living systems, for example), could be explained using chemical structures and chemical equations.

These examples are only a sampling of the work done in the 1920s by chemists attempting to understand the structure and function of biologically important molecules. A number of other significant results could also be cited. In 1929, for example, the Russian-American chemist Phoebus Levene discovered the presence of the sugar deoxyribose in certain types of nucleic acids. These substances, deoxyribonucleic acid, or DNA, were later shown to be the material in which genetic information is stored in biochemical molecules.

3

LIFE SCIENCES

The 1920s was a decade during which important developments took place in both theoretical biology and the applied health sciences. Biologists for the first time began to see on a molecular basis how hereditary changes are transmitted from one generation to another, and they made critical discoveries about the origin of the human species. In addition, research began to reveal the crucial role of vitamins, antibiotics, and other substances in the maintenance of good health.

VITAMINS AND HEALTH

The role of vitamins in maintaining the health of an organism was first recognized by the Dutch physician Christiaan Eijkman in the late 1890s. During the 1920s, important new information about four of these essential trace substances in the body—vitamins C, D, E, and niacin—was uncovered.

One of the most active contributors to this line of research was the American biochemist Elmer Verner McCollum. McCollum studied the functions of vitamins A and B during the 1910s and then in the 1920s switched his attention to vitamins D and E. In 1922, McCollum and his colleagues at the Johns Hopkins University School of Hygiene and Public Health in Baltimore, Maryland, found that a form of cod-liver oil was able to cure a very old and horrible disease, rickets. They gave the name *vitamin D* to that substance and then analyzed a number of foods to determine the amount of the vitamin each contained. One consequence of this research was that a cure became available for rickets.

McCollum was also involved in pioneering research on vitamin E, although credit for the actual discovery of that substance is usually given to

Today, vitamin E is available in tablet form and is often taken as a nutritional supplement.

American researchers Herbert Evans and K. J. Scott. In 1922, Evans and Scott found that rats that are deprived of certain foods—especially leafy green vegetables and cereal grains—produce fewer offspring. They suggested that this result was due to a lack of some fertility-promoting substance present in those foods. A year later, the biochemist B. Sure suggested the name *vitamin E* for the fertility-promoting factor found by Evans and Scott. He also identified a number of other foods in which the vitamin could be found.

Preliminary work on two more vitamins also began in the 1920s. The American physician Joseph Goldberger spent most of his professional career trying to find the cause of the disease known as pellagra. In the early twentieth century, pellagra was widespread in the United States, especially among poor people in the southern states. Thousands of people died each year from the disease, and many more were afflicted with skin and digestive disorders and with the delirium that characterizes the disease.

Goldberger was convinced that pellagra was caused by the deficiency of some substance in a person's diet. By conducting a long series of experiments, Goldberger was able to isolate a substance that could cure the disease. In 1928, he named that substance the P-P (for pellagra-preventing) factor. Goldberger himself died the following year and so did not witness the 1932 discovery that the P-P factor is actually nicotinic acid, a vitamin more commonly known today as niacin.

Initial work leading to the discovery of yet another vitamin was announced in 1928 by the Hungarian-American biochemist Albert Szent-Györgyi. Szent-Györgyi discovered a compound containing six carbon atoms to which he gave the name *hexuronic acid*. The compound occurred abundantly in cabbages and oranges and proved to be effective in treating the symptoms of scurvy.

Dr. Joseph Goldberger identified the substance, now known as niacin, that cures pellagra.

Scurvy is a disease that had plagued human civilization for centuries. It is characterized by swollen and bleeding gums, bruises on the skin, and extreme weakness. The disease was once very common among sailors. In 1747, a British naval officer by the name of James Lind discovered that feeding sailors citrus fruits such as oranges, lemons, and limes greatly reduced their tendency to develop scurvy. From that discovery came the common name by which British sailors are still known: "limeys."

Szent-Györgyi suspected that hexuronic acid might be the antiscurvy agent that Lind had discovered. By the time Szent-Györgyi felt confident enough to actually announce his opinion in 1932, however, a similar report by American biochemist Charles King had preceded him by only two weeks. The compound discovered by Szent-Györgyi and King is now known as vitamin C or ascorbic acid.

Oranges, and other citrus fruits, are among the primary sources of vitamin C.

OTHER IMPORTANT BIOCHEMICALS

Research on vitamins in the 1920s led to cures for a number of disorders that had plagued humans through the years. Other discoveries during the decade increased the number of disorders that could be treated by medical science. Probably the most famous of these discoveries was that made by two Canadian physiologists, Sir Frederick Banting and Charles Best.

Banting and Best worked on one of the most widespread and debilitating of all human disorders, diabetes. Diabetes results from the body's inability to break down sugar in the body properly. It is generally accompanied by a number of symptoms such as weight loss and increase in appetite and often results in coma and death. By 1920, scientists had learned that diabetes was involved in some way with a malfunction of the pancreas.

In 1921, Banting had become convinced that a specific portion of the pancreas, the islets of Langerhans, produces a substance that would combat diabetes. He obtained permission from John J. R. Macleod, professor of physiology at the University of Toronto, to use some of his laboratory space to test his ideas. He also recruited Best, a medical student at the time, to assist in the research.

By late 1921, Banting and Best had accomplished their objective. They had isolated a substance—insulin—that reversed the symptoms of diabetes. They had demonstrated that the compound cured the disorder in dogs and then, in January 1922, they tried it for the first time with a human volunteer, a diabetic boy by the name of Leonard Thompson. Almost immediately, Leonard showed rapid improvement from the treatment.

Banting and Best's achievement has led to relief for untold millions of diabetics. For this accomplishment, the Nobel Prize in physiology or medicine for 1923 was awarded to Banting and, strangely enough, Macleod. In one of the most famous slights in the history of this prestigious award, Best was ignored by the Nobel Prize committee.

Simultaneously with the work of Banting and Best, a trio of American physicians was working on another serious disease, pernicious anemia. Pernicious anemia is a condition in which the body fails to produce a sufficient number of red blood corpuscles (cells), eventually resulting in a person's death. In 1917, George Hoyt Whipple at the University of California at Berkeley began a series of experiments aimed at finding out how red blood corpuscles are formed in the body. He bled a group of dogs and then studied them to see which foods produced the greatest rejuvenation of red blood cells. He found that liver was the most potent of the foods he tried.

Whipple's results became the motivation for another series of studies, by the American physicians George Minot and William Murphy in 1924. Minot and Murphy fed patients ill with pernicious anemia diets high in liver. They found that the treatment worked very well and that all patients recovered completely. For this work, Whipple, Minot, and Murphy were jointly awarded

Sir Frederick Banting (right) and Charles Best (left). Their discovery that insulin cured diabetes in dogs led to relief for millions of human diabetics.

THE EXODUS FROM GERMANY

In 1920, Germany was indisputably one of the world's great—if not the greatest—scientific powers. Two decades later, the nation's scientific community was in shambles. The vast majority of its most important members had fled the madness of Adolf Hitler's rising power. Even a half century after Hitler's destruction in World War II, the nation has yet to recover from the anti-intellectualism and hatred of non-Aryans promoted by the Nazi Party.

Among dozens of dramatic stories that could be told of the period, that of Otto Loewi is typical. In 1921, Loewi discovered a material that seemed to be released during the stimulation of a nerve. Originally called *vagusstoffe* ("vagus stuff") by Loewi, the substance was later renamed acetylcholine by the English biologist Henry Dale. Acetylcholine was the first of many compounds known as neurotransmitters (compounds that are responsible for the passage of electrical messages throughout the body) to be discovered.

Loewi shared the 1936 Nobel Prize for physiology or medicine with Dale and then, only two years later, was placed under arrest by the Nazi government in Austria. He was allowed to leave his native land only after turning over his Nobel Prize money to the German government. He spent the last two decades of his life in the United States.

the 1934 Nobel Prize for physiology or medicine. The substance in liver that protects against pernicious anemia was later identified as vitamin B_{12}.

A third breakthrough in the health sciences occurred in 1928 with the discovery of penicillin by the Scottish bacteriologist Alexander Fleming. That event is often used as an example of the way in which accidents can result in important scientific breakthroughs. In this case, Fleming was about to clean out a petri dish containing staphylococcus bacteria that he had been studying some days earlier. Just before doing so, however, he noticed spots on the dish where bacteria had died off.

Rather than ignoring this observation and continuing with his cleanup, Fleming decided to find out how the bacteria had been killed. He was able to determine that spores from the mold known as *Penicillium notatum* had accidentally fallen into the dish. At each point where a mold had landed, bacteria had been killed off.

Fleming hypothesized that the mold released some substance that was toxic to bacteria, an "antibiotic." He quickly realized the potential medical benefit of such a material and carried out tests to determine its safety in use with humans. The successful conclusion of those tests eventually led to the

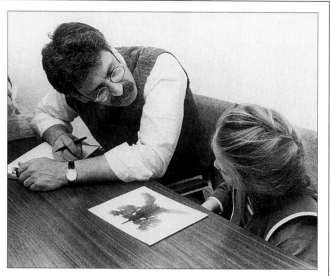
use of penicillin as the world's first commercial antibiotic. Fleming himself was not able to reach this final goal, however. Indeed, it was not until the early 1940s that final tests of penicillin were completed and the drug was put into production.

ADVANCES IN THEORETICAL BIOLOGY

As progress was going forward in the health sciences, biologists were also making a number of critical discoveries about the fundamental nature of living organisms. Some of the most important breakthroughs in the 1920s took place in the field of genetics.

Some biologists have said that the key question in all of the life sciences is how hereditary information is stored within an organism and how that information is then transmitted from one generation to the next. One of the most influential biologists working in this area in the 1920s was the American geneticist Thomas Hunt Morgan.

The red-eyed fruit fly, Drosophila

Early in his career, Morgan decided to use the fruit fly *Drosophila* for his research subject. The organism has only four chromosomes, reproduces every few days, and is, therefore, relatively simple to study. For more than three decades, Morgan studied the changes that took place over hundreds of *Drosophila* generations.

The key element in these studies was the presence of mutations, changes that take place in an organism's characteristics from one generation to the next. The presence of a mutation allowed Morgan to decide what part of a chromosome was responsible for each of the fruit fly's characteristics. By the late 1910s, he had published the first of his chromosome maps summarizing his findings.

During the 1920s, Morgan drew a number of conclusions about the mechanisms by which hereditary characteristics are transmitted, conclusions described in his 1926 book *The Theory of the Gene.* According to Morgan, an organism's characteristics are determined by specific genes that are arranged in a linear sequence along a chromosome. These genes are usually transmitted as a group during reproduction, but changes may occur when chromosomes cross over and recombine or when a chromosome is damaged in some way or another.

Within a year of the publication of Morgan's book, one of his students had provided new insight into the cause of at least some kinds of mutations. The American biologist Hermann J. Muller had been exploring the effect of X rays on *Drosophila.* In 1927, he reported that the number of mutations increased more than a hundredfold among fruit flies that had been exposed

Thomas Hunt Morgan is seen here, apparently signing autographs for young fans—most unusual for a scientist!

to radiation. Muller's discovery was important because it demonstrated that mutations are not unexplainable random events, but are often the result of specific and identifiable external causes.

HUMAN ANCESTRY

Just as humans change from generation to generation, so does the human species evolve from millennium to millennium. The 1920s was a decade during which anthropologists made some key discoveries about the history of our species. The first of these discoveries was announced on February 3, 1925, by the Australian-South African anthropologist Raymond A. Dart. A

THE SCOPES TRIAL

The publication of Charles Darwin's works on evolution in the mid-nineteenth century unleashed a storm of controversy that continues today. At the core of the controversy is the debate over the origin of the human species. Throughout this period, conservative religious denominations have insisted that human evolution is theologically incorrect, and they have fought vigorously to prevent it from being taught in the public schools.

In 1925, John T. Scopes, a biology teacher from Dayton, Tennessee, volunteered to be arrested for violating a state law forbidding the teaching of evolution. The trial that followed, sometimes called the Monkey Trial, is widely regarded as one of the most important court events of the twentieth century. In that trial, the famous criminal lawyer Clarence Darrow was in charge of Scopes's defense team, while three-time candidate for president of the United States William Jennings Bryan was the lead prosecutor.

The trial lasted for eleven days in one of the hottest summers in Tennessee history. The high point of the trial came when Darrow called Bryan to the witness stand. In his questions, the famous defense attorney made the brilliant Bryan look like something of a fool. Darrow was not able to save his client, however, since Scopes had admitted to breaking the law. As a result, Scopes was convicted and fined $100. Sometime later, the verdict was reversed on a technical point. The story of the Scopes trial was later made into a popular motion picture, *Inherit the Wind*.

The Scopes case in Tennessee was only the most famous of many battles going on between science and religion in the United States in the 1920s. For example, in 1925, the Texas State Board of Education made a ruling that forbade the use of any textbook in which evolution was discussed. The dispute about the place of evolutionary science in the schools has never really disappeared from American society. Religious conservatives in the 1990s continue to fight the same battle that so disrupted Tennessee, Texas, and other states in the 1920s.

limestone quarry near Taung, not far from Johannesburg, had yielded the skull of an organism never seen before, Dart said. It was an organism that he described as "intermediate between living anthropoids and man." Dart suggested the name *Australopithecus africanus* ("ape man from the south") for the new species.

Dart's announcement was greeted with derision and amusement by many of his colleagues and the general public. But he persevered in his search for other examples of *Australopithecus*. It took the better part of two decades for him to find enough additional specimens to convince even his severest critics that his find was an important new addition to the story of human evolution.

Raymond A. Dart, with the original specimen of Australopithecus africanus

At about the same time that Dart was searching for fossils of early humans in South Africa, a similar search was taking place in China. A leading figure of the Chinese research activities was the Swedish paleontologist Otto Zdansky. Zdansky was hired by the Swedish Paleontological Institute of Uppsala to follow up on earlier reports of fossilized teeth thought possibly to belong to an early humanoid animal.

Zdansky arrived at the village of Chou K'ou-Tien, near Peking (present-day Beijing), in 1921, but he had little success in his excavations until two years later. Then he found a single molar in an area known as Dragon Bone Hill. Zdansky made no mention of his find until 1926, however, when a colleague announced to the world that evidence for a primitive form of human had been found in China.

One of the first scientists to hear of Zdansky's find was the Canadian anthropologist Davidson Black. Black had long been convinced that the human species arose in Asia. He was delighted, therefore, when he was offered a position at the Peking Union Medical College in 1920. For a number of years, his own research for human ancestors went nowhere. But news of Zdansky's find in 1926 renewed his enthusiasm for the search. In fact, he

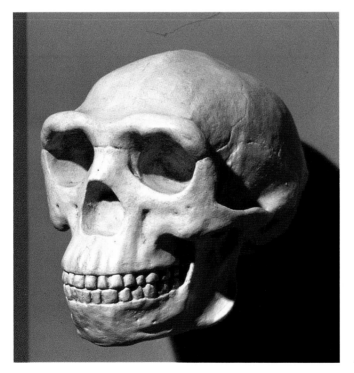

A skull of Peking man

boldly wrote at the time that "the actual presence of early man in Eastern Asia is no longer a matter of conjecture." He even offered a name for Zdansky's discovery: *Sinanthropus Pekinensis* ("Chinese man of Peking").

At this point, Black decided to approach the Rockefeller Foundation for the financing needed to carry out a massive excavation of the region around Chou K'ou-Tien. The foundation responded favorably and digging got under way. Since Zdansky had by this time accepted an appointment at Cairo University, in Egypt, the new project director was another Swedish paleontologist, Birger Bohlin.

In December 1929, the expedition struck gold: one of Black's assistants, Weng Chung Pei, found an almost complete skull of Peking man. The individual had lived more than a half million years earlier, one of the earliest and best-preserved examples of human ancestors to have been found at the time.

Research during the 1920s also began to reveal more about the more recent history of our species. Two of the most important events took place in 1922. In the first of these, the English archaeologist Charles Leonard Woolley began his excavation of the ancient city of Ur, along the lower part of the Euphrates River. Ur is mentioned in the Bible and was probably the most important city of Sumer, the world's first civilized state.

In the same year, an archaeological expedition led by George E. S. M. Herbert and Howard Carter of England discovered the tomb of Tutankhamen in Egypt. The eighteen-year-old pharaoh's tomb was probably the most spectacular find ever made by archaeologists. By custom, the pharaohs of ancient Egypt had been buried in incredibly elaborate tombs deep within pyramids. In spite of the architectural obstacles involved, as well as the threat of curses, grave robbers had broken into and looted every one of the ancient tombs save one, that of Tutankhamen, a young man who is thought to have ruled Egypt from 1361 to 1352 B.C.

When Herbert and Carter discovered Tutankhamen's tomb, they could scarcely believe the riches it contained. It held a wealth of gold, jewels, and other treasures. The king himself was buried within the innermost of three coffins. That coffin was made of solid gold. Wrapped in the mummy's burial clothes were an additional 143 pieces of precious jewelry. The discovery made by Herbert and Carter holds fascination for specialists and amateurs

The discovery of King Tutankhamen's tomb, filled with artifacts like this mask, was one of the most spectacular finds in the history of archaeology.

alike even seven decades later. Each of the 1922 discoveries stimulated interest in early human civilizations among both professional archaeologists and the general public.

ADVANCES IN MEDICAL TECHNOLOGY

Throughout the 1920s, techniques and instruments for the treatment of medical problems continued to improve. Three of the most important of these were invented toward the end of the decade: the Pap test, the iron lung, and the electroencephalograph.

The Pap test for uterine cancer was announced in 1928 by the Greek-American physician George N. Papanicolaou. For more than a decade, Papanicolaou had been studying reproductive cycles in the female guinea pig and in humans. In the course of these studies, he happened to notice that cells obtained from women with cancer of the cervix had an unusual appearance. He decided that this discovery might provide a way of predicting the presence of cervical cancer in women with early stages of the disease, before it became a more serious condition. The "Pap test" developed by Papanicolaou is now widely used to test for the presence of cervical and uterine cancer in women.

Papanicolaou's discovery would appear to have been a major breakthrough in cancer diagnosis. At the time, uterine cancer was the second most common cause of death among women in the United States. Use of the Pap test made it possible to detect the presence of the disease long before visible symptoms appeared. Under such conditions, the cure rate for women with the disease could be expected to reach at least 80 percent.

Unfortunately, Papanicolaou's colleagues were not impressed by his discovery and largely ignored it. Only in the 1940s, with the publication of *Diagnosis of Uterine Cancer* by Papanicolaou and Herbert Trant, was the test's value fully appreciated by the medical profession. It received full validation in 1948 when the American Cancer Society recommended the Pap test for all women on a regular basis.

Progress in the treatment of a second major disease occurred in 1929 when the American engineer Philip Drinker invented the iron lung. The lung is a machine that helps patients with poliomyelitis to breathe. Poliomyelitis

is caused by a virus that attacks the central nervous system and causes various types of paralysis. In many instances, paralysis strikes the respiratory muscles and makes it difficult or impossible for a person to breathe on his or her own. Death by suffocation can then occur within hours.

The iron lung consists of an airtight metal casing into which the patient is placed. A mechanical blower then forces air into the lungs, taking over the patient's respiration for her or him. Untold thousands of lives were saved in the thirty years following the machine's invention. Then, in the 1950s, the discovery of the Salk and Sabin vaccines first offered protection from poliomyelitis, and the need for the iron lung dropped dramatically.

A second major invention in 1929 was the electroencephalograph (EEG), made by the German psychiatrist Hans Berger. Berger's interest was in finding the relationship that exists between physical changes in the brain and mental processes. What kinds of physical changes take place within the

INVENTION OF THE POLYGRAPH

Efforts to design a device that would measure the truthfulness of suspected criminals go back to the late nineteenth century. The famous criminologist Cesare Lombroso built an instrument that measured a subject's blood pressure and heart rate during questioning. The device was based on the well-known fact that a person's body functions often undergo dramatic change during a time of stress, as when he or she is lying.

Improvements on Lombroso's concept were constructed in succeeding decades, most successfully by John Larson in 1921. Larson was a police officer in Berkeley, California, when he built the first modern polygraph. Larson's

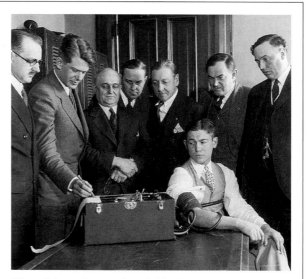

Use of the polygraph quickly became part of police procedure. A suspect is being tested in this photograph, taken in 1931.

device measured blood pressure, heart rate, and electrical conductivity of the skin of a subject during questioning. It received its first practical test in the identification of a University of California student suspected of shoplifting in 1921. The polygraph rapidly became a popular tool for the investigation of crime. But many serious questions remain about how accurate the machine is and how the results it produces can best be used.

human brain, he wondered, when a person has an idea, learns a new fact, recalls a previous event, or performs some other mental function.

Berger's first research involved measurements of changes in brain size and brain temperature during mental processes. But his results were discouraging, and he turned his attention to electrical changes in the brain that accompany mental processes. This line of research had been pioneered in the 1870s by the English physiologist Richard Caton, who had developed a method for measuring the brain waves produced in monkeys and rabbits.

In 1924, Berger first measured electrical signals resulting from brain activity in a human subject. His results were unclear, however, and he spent another five years perfecting his machine and technique. In 1929, Berger published the first of what was to become a series of fifteen papers on the electroencephalogram technique. Although he recognized the need for continued

A readout from a modern electroencephalograph. Hans Berger's invention is used widely today.

improvement of his instrument, Berger also had confidence that the EEG would become a useful tool for the diagnosis of malfunctions of the brain. He was correct in that hope and belief, and the EEG has become one of the most widely used instruments in neurophysiology today.

4

EARTH AND SPACE SCIENCES

The 1920s was a decade in which scientists learned crucial new facts about the most distant parts of our universe and the deepest parts of our own planet. One common feature of these studies was an increased realization of the role of change in the natural world. Whether gazing at distant stars and galaxies or examining the ocean depths, scientists were continuously confirmed in their view that earth and outer space are constantly evolving.

THE PROPERTIES OF STARS

Technological developments in astronomy during the early twentieth century began to pay large dividends in the 1920s. The 100-inch (250-centimeter) Mount Wilson telescope, put into operation in 1917, began to reveal features of the sky never seen in such detail before. One of the first of these discoveries was reported in 1920 by the American physicist Albert Michelson. Using a 20-foot (6-meter) light-measuring device of his own design in conjunction with the Mount Wilson telescope, Michelson was able to measure the diameter of the red giant star Alpha Orionis (Betelgeuse). He accomplished this amazing feat by measuring the angle made by light rays coming from opposite sides of the star. Michelson reported the star's diameter to be about 260 million miles (420 million kilometers).

Discoveries like Michelson's also made possible new theoretical insights into the nature of stars. Two of the most important of these were Eddington's mass-luminosity law and theories on the production of energy in stars.

The English astronomer Sir Arthur Eddington made some of his most important contributions in explaining how stars hold together. Two important forces are at work in this process. One is the force of gravity, which tends to pull the materials the star is made of toward its center. The other is

The constellation Orion. The bright star near top left is Betelgeuse, a red giant star 600 light years away from earth.

an outward pressure resulting from energy released by the star. This pressure tends to blow the star apart. Eddington showed how the balance of these two contrasting forces could be used to calculate the interior temperature of a star.

An additional consequence of this work was Eddington's discovery of the effect of a star's mass on its luminosity (brightness). In 1924, Eddington showed that the luminosity of a star varies with the star's mass. That is, the heavier a star is, the brighter it tends to be.

Throughout the 1920s, scientists from many disciplines wrestled with the question of how stars produce energy. It was obvious that no familiar mechanism such as combustion (burning) could account for the enormous amounts of energy released by a star. Toward the end of the decade, an important breakthrough took place. The Russian-American physicist George Gamow suggested that stellar energy is formed when hydrogen nuclei fuse (combine) with each other to form a helium nucleus. Gamow argued that in some still unknown way, this fusion process would result in the release of energy in the quantities actually observed in stars. Gamow's theory was remarkable (and later shown to be essentially correct) because very little was then known about any type of nuclear reaction, including nuclear fusion.

George Gamow contributed to the field of astronomy for years. Here, he is talking with college students in 1954.

GALAXIES AND AN EXPANDING UNIVERSE

Some of the most spectacular work done with the 100-inch (250-centimeter) Mount Wilson telescope was that carried out by the American astronomer Edwin Hubble. Hubble began work at the Mount Wilson Observatory at the end of World War II and remained there for the rest of his professional life. The subject he originally turned his attention to was the nature of nebulae, which had first been investigated by the French astronomer Charles Messier in the late 1700s. By 1920, astronomers were still largely uncertain about the composition and actual location of these objects in the sky. Some scientists thought that nebulae were clouds of gas and dust, while others believed that they were enormous collections of stars. Also, some people said that the nebulae lay within our own Milky Way, and others argued that they were outside its boundaries.

In 1924, Hubble announced the first of many breakthroughs regarding nebulae. He had been able to locate a dozen Cepheid variable stars in the Andromeda nebula. Cepheid variable stars are stars whose brightness changes according to a very regular schedule. They go from very bright to very dim and then back again, in a pattern that astronomers have measured quite accurately.

The importance of this discovery was that a method for determining distances based on Cepheids had been developed by the American astronomer Henrietta Leavitt in 1912. Using this method, Hubble calculated that the

Edwin Hubble, one of the major contributors to the field of modern astronomy

Andromeda nebula was about 750,000 light-years from earth. (He later found that his original estimate was far too low.) That distance placed the nebula far beyond the outer limits of the Milky Way and confirmed that it was a large collection of stars much like our own galaxy.

Throughout the decade, Hubble continued to add information about galaxies (a term originally suggested by Harlow Shapley). He proposed a system for classifying galaxies according to their shape: spiral, elliptical, or irregular. He also confirmed current opinion that the vast majority of galaxies consist of huge numbers of stars, just as the Milky Way does. Hubble once estimated that the number of galaxies in the universe is probably at least as great as the number of stars in our Milky Way.

Hubble's final accomplishment of the decade—and one of his most important—came in 1929. He began with the earlier work of the American astronomer Vesto Slipher. Slipher had made many measurements on the radial velocity of galaxies, the speed at which they seem to be traveling away from the earth. Hubble used Slipher's measurements and then added many more of his own to determine the distance of various galaxies from the earth and the rate at which they were receding from our planet. He found a direct relationship between these two quantities that says that the faster a galaxy is moving away from the earth, the farther away it is. Hubble's law, as the relationship is commonly called, provided astronomers with a powerful new tool for measuring distances in outer space beyond those for which the Cepheid variable system was valid.

Hubble's research on galaxies had provided critical confirmation for the

---

KONSTANTIN TSIOLKOVSKY (1857–1935)

Few Americans are likely to recognize the name of Konstantin Tsiolkovsky. Yet Tsiolkovsky is undoubtedly one of the great figures in the early history of space science. Born to a poor family in a remote region of Russia in 1857, Tsiolkovsky was essentially self-taught in science. He once wrote that "there were very few books [when he was growing up], and I had no teachers at all. . . . I had to figure out everything by myself."

Still, Tsiolkovsky developed a number of the early principles of space flight, many of which were published in the 1920s. In 1957, the Soviet Union scheduled the launch of *Sputnik I*, the world's first artificial earth satellite, to coincide with the hundredth anniversary of Tsiolkovsky's birth. The launch failed to meet that date, but by only a matter of weeks.

concept of an expanding universe. The Dutch astronomer Willem de Sitter had been an early follower of Albert Einstein's theory of relativity. De Sitter had demonstrated on purely theoretical grounds that Einstein's theory suggested a universe that is constantly expanding, like an enlarging soap bubble. The final details of that theory were worked out in 1922 by the Russian mathematician Alexsandr Friedmann. It was not until Hubble's work on galaxies, however, that the theories of de Sitter and Friedmann received final proof. The Hubble Space Telescope, launched in 1990 by the National Aeronautics and Space Administration, was named in Hubble's honor.

COSMOLOGY

The concept of an expanding universe suggests one important conclusion that many scientists found somewhat troubling. If the universe truly is spreading out over time, then there must have been a moment at some time in the past when everything the universe is made of was concentrated in a single point. The spreading ripples on a lake, for comparison, are concrete evidence of the fact that some object must have fallen into the water earlier to cause the ripples.

The first detailed theory of the universe's origin was worked out in 1927 by the Belgian astronomer Abbé Georges Lemaître. Lemaître argued that one could use data on the expansion rate of galaxies to calculate backward to a time when they were all located in a single point. In a sense, he was suggesting that scientists should be able to run a motion picture of the history of the universe in reverse and see what took place at the very beginning of the film. Lemaître hypothesized that the "film" (the history of the universe) began about two billion years ago. At that point, he said, all matter in the universe existed in the form of a "cosmic egg" or "superatom." At the instant of creation, all of that matter was released from the cosmic egg in a "big bang." Lemaître's theory basically matches the scenario today's scientists believe for the creation of the universe, although they now set the date of the big bang much earlier than the time chosen by Lemaître.

Lemaître's theory received little attention when it was first announced. Six years later, however, it was featured in a book by Sir Arthur Eddington, *The Expanding Universe*, which summarized all that was currently known on the subject. The book was an exciting and fitting climax to an eventful decade of astronomical and cosmological research.

THE EARTH'S ATMOSPHERE

The origins of modern weather-forecasting techniques can be traced to the work of a Norwegian father-and-son team, Vilhelm and Jacob Bjerknes, in the 1920s. During World War I, the Bjerkneses had established an extensive system of weather observation stations throughout Norway. From the data collected at these stations, they discovered a number of elements that are used in weather forecasting today.

For example, the Bjerkneses learned of the existence of large pockets of air that are significantly warmer or cooler than the surrounding atmosphere. In a 1920 publication, they called these regions warm air masses and cold air masses. The Bjerkneses also found that certain weather patterns could be associated with the boundary between a warm air mass and a cold air mass. They referred to these boundaries as fronts. This information is the starting point from which weather forecasts are still made today.

Another line of research on the atmosphere also resulted from World War I activities. In England, Edward Appleton had spent the war years in the Royal Engineers as a radio officer. He had become intrigued with the problem of fading radio signals, which often occurred at night. After the war, he decided to continue research on this question.

Appleton had the idea that radio signals sent out from one place on the earth traveled into the air, were somehow reflected by the atmosphere, and returned to the earth at another location. The process he had in mind was somewhat similar to bouncing a tennis ball off a ceiling at an angle.

In 1924, Appleton persuaded the British Broadcasting Corporation (BBC) to let him use its radio signals after the network had closed down at the end of the day. He and a graduate student, Miles Barnett, projected the BBC's radio signal into the atmosphere. Then they searched for places around the country where they could pick up that same radio signal. By measuring the angles at which the radio signal went into the atmosphere and bounced back, Appleton and Barnett were able to locate a layer about 60 miles (100 kilometers) up in the atmosphere from which radio waves are reflected.

That layer was later called the E layer, part of the Heaviside-Kennelly layer, named in honor of two electrical engineers who had predicted its existence some years earlier. In 1926, Appleton discovered a second reflecting layer about 150 miles (240 kilometers) above the earth's surface. That layer later became known as the F or Appleton layer, in honor of its discoverer.

Appleton continued his study of the atmosphere throughout the decade. In 1927, he observed changes in the E and F layers during a solar eclipse and became convinced that the changes are produced by solar radiation. Appleton's discoveries later became crucial to the development of radio, radar, television, and other forms of communication.

One of the most ingenious experiments conducted on the earth's atmosphere in the 1920s was that of British physicist Frederick Alexander Lindemann and his colleague, meteorologist G. M. B. Dobson. The pair found a way to estimate the temperature of the upper ranges of the atmosphere, far beyond the limits of sounding balloons then used to make such measurements. Their method consisted of analyzing the characteristics of meteor trails in the upper atmosphere. They worked out a procedure for calculating the temperature of the region of space through which a meteor passed based on the brightness and length of its tail.

Their results were startling. Lindemann and Dobson suggested that temperatures at an altitude of about 30 miles (50 kilometers) were about 70°F (20°C), far warmer than the value of -60°F (-50°C) then accepted by scientists. Until the work of Lindemann and Dobson, scientists had assumed that tem-

The power of a cosmic ray is shown in this false-color photograph taken in 1950.

peratures continued to decrease as one goes higher in the atmosphere. It was to be more than ten years before the discovery of an ozone layer in the upper stratosphere provided an explanation for this temperature inconsistency.

The 1920s was also a period during which extensive studies of cosmic radiation in the earth's atmosphere were carried out. Cosmic radiation is radiation somewhat like X rays that reaches the earth's atmosphere from outer space. Cosmic rays had first been observed by the Swiss physicist Albert Gockel in 1910. They were then studied more intensively during the rest of that decade by the Austrian physicist Victor Franz Hess. In 1921, the American physicist Robert Andrews Millikan became interested in cosmic rays and was actually the first to suggest that they be called by this name.

Millikan's work was sparked by a controversy then raging through the field of atmospheric physics about the origin of cosmic rays. Some researchers thought the radiation originated from radioactive materials in the earth's crust. Others believed that the rays traveled to the earth from some distant source outside our solar system. Millikan designed and carried out a series of experiments to test these two hypotheses. He sent electroscopes high into the atmosphere and deep into lakes at many locations throughout the United States. He finally came to the conclusion that cosmic rays come not from the earth but from space, thus explaining the name he chose for them.

OCEANOGRAPHIC RESEARCH

Scientists often comment about the fact that they probably know more about the moon and the planets in our solar system than they do about the depths of the earth's oceans. That statement was certainly true in 1920, although some important breakthroughs were to occur in the decade to follow. Probably the most significant of these events was the voyage of the German research vessel *Meteor* across the Atlantic Ocean in 1925.

That voyage was originally planned by the German government as an attempt to find out whether gold could be extracted from seawater. Germany had been assessed very large financial penalties after losing World War I and hoped to find a new source of income with which to pay off those penalties.

The project was placed under the command of Alfred Merz, a well-known geographer. Merz became ill during the voyage, however, and was replaced by George Wüst, who was to become one of the most famous oceanographers of his day. One of Wüst's best-known accomplishments was his four-volume work *Results of German Atlantic Expedition "METEOR,"* published between 1925 and 1927.

The primary goal of the *Meteor* expedition came to naught as it soon became apparent that the concentration of gold in seawater was too low for economical recovery. But a secondary goal—mapping the ocean bottom—proved far more successful. As the ship moved around the Atlantic Ocean for more than two years, it took echo soundings every 2 to 3 miles (3 to 5 kilometers) on its 42,000-mile (68,000-kilometer) trip. These soundings made possible the first detailed map of ocean floor topography.

The most significant discovery during the mapping was the presence of an elevated section of land later given the name the Midatlantic Ridge. The ridge is a gigantic submerged mountain range extending a total length of more than 10,000 miles (16,000 kilometers) down the center of the Atlantic Ocean.

Merz and Wüst had also been involved in extensive studies of circulation patterns in the Atlantic Ocean a few years earlier. By measuring temperature and salinity (saltiness) of seawater in many different locations, they were able to map massive currents flowing at various levels of the ocean. In 1922, they reported the presence of a northward flow of water at surface levels, a southward flow at depths ranging from 0.5 to 2.5 miles (0.8 to 4 kilometers), and another northward flow at deeper levels.

After completing his research on the *Meteor*, Wüst turned his attention to the Pacific Ocean. There he mapped ocean currents as he had done for the Atlantic a few years earlier. In 1929, he reported the results of that research. The major difference between the two oceans, he said, was the absence of cross-equatorial currents in the Pacific similar to those he and Merz had found in the Atlantic.

The year 1929 also marked the publication of another major work on ocean circulation, *The Circulation of the Indian Ocean,* by the German oceanographer Lisa Moller. Moller found a three-level pattern of circulation in the Indian Ocean similar to that reported by Merz and Wüst for the Atlantic seven years earlier.

Given the limitations of their equipment, Merz, Wüst, Moller, and their colleagues made some remarkable discoveries about the planet's oceans. Not until the massive research studies of the 1957–1958 International Geophysical Year were these discoveries significantly updated.

Further Reading

Aaseng, Nathan. *Charles Darwin: Revolutionary Biologist*. Minneapolis: Lerner Publications, 1993.

Asimov, Isaac. *How Did We Find Out About Our Genes?* New York: Walker and Co., 1983.

_____. *How Did We Find Out About Vitamins?* New York: Walker and Co., 1974.

Biel, Timothy Levi. *Atoms: Building Blocks of Matter*. San Diego: Greenhaven, 1990.

Blake, Arthur. *The Scopes Trial: Defending the Right to Teach*. Brookfield, C.T.: Millbrook Press, 1994.

Byczynski, Lynn. *Genetics: Nature's Blueprints*. San Diego: Lucent Books, 1991.

Kaye, Judith. *The Life of Alexander Fleming*. New York: Twenty-First Century Books, 1993.

Landau, Elaine. *Diabetes*. New York: Twenty-First Century Books, 1994.

Lye, Keith. *The Ocean Floor*. New York: Franklin Watts, 1991.

Newton, David. *The Chemical Elements*. New York: Franklin Watts, 1994.

_____. *Linus Pauling: Scientist and Advocate*. New York: Facts on File, 1994.

Parker, Steve. *Charles Darwin and Evolution*. New York: HarperCollins Children's Books, 1992.

Reeves, Nicholas. *Into the Mummy's Tomb: The Real-Life Discovery of Tutankhamun's Treasures*. New York: Scholastic Inc., 1992.

Reiff, Stephanie A. *Secrets of Tut's Tomb and the Pyramids*. Austin, T.X.: Raintree/Steck-Vaughn Publishers, 1983.

Silverstein, Alvin, et al. *Diabetes*. Springfield, N.J.: Enslow Publishers, 1994.

_____. *Vitamins and Minerals*. Brookfield, C.T.: Millbrook Press, 1992.

Streissguth, Tom. *Rocket Man: The Story of Robert Goddard*. Minneapolis: Carolrhoda, 1995.

Tames, Richard. *Alexander Fleming*. New York: Franklin Watts, 1990.

Whitelaw, Nancy. *Margaret Sanger: Every Child a Wanted Child*. New York: Dillon, 1994.

Index

About the Author

David E. Newton has a bachelor of science degree in chemistry and a masters degree in education from the University of Michigan and a doctorate in science education from Harvard University. Over the past four decades, he has taught courses in chemistry, physical science, human sexuality, teacher education, science and social issues, and other topics from grade 3 to graduate school.

Dr. Newton is the author of more than 400 books and other educational publications. Some of his most recent books for young readers include *Global Warming*, *The Gay and Lesbian Rights Movement*, *The Ozone Dilemma*, *Alan Turing: A Biography*, *Teen Violence*, *Gun Control: An Issue for the 1990s*, *Hunting*, and *Linus Pauling: Scientist and Advocate*. The last three of these books have been recognized with New York Public Library Book of the Year awards for 1993, 1994, and 1995.

Dr. Newton is currently a full-time writer and full-time innkeeper in Ashland, Oregon. In his spare time, he is responsible for the goats, ducks, geese, rabbits, cats, and dog at the inn, as well as for maintaining the quarter acre garden there.